# Artlist Collection
# THE DOG
## Guide to Life

W9-ALV-028

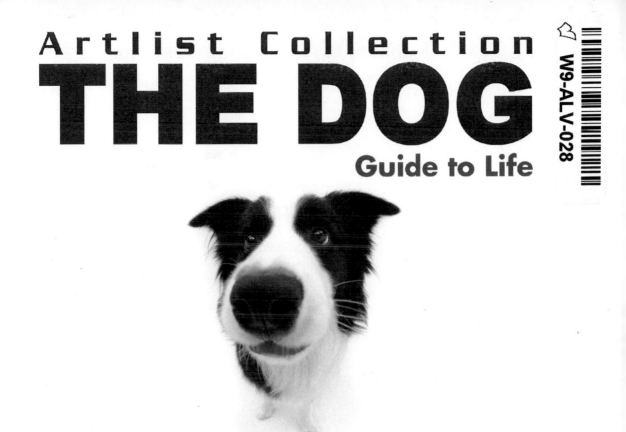

**Translated by Howie Dewin**
**Original text by The Dogs**

SCHOLASTIC INC.

New York     Toronto     London     Auckland     Sydney
Mexico City     New Delhi     Hong Kong     Buenos Aires

Special thanks to top dog Howie Dewin for knowing that our bark is worse than our bite!
— The Dogs

ISBN 0-439-72211-X

4Kids Entertainment/THE DOG is a registered trademark of and © artlist INTERNATIONAL.

12 11 10 9 8 7 6 5 4 3 2          5 6 7 8 9/0

Designed by Stephen Hughes
Printed in the U.S.A.
First printing, January 2005

If a picture wasn't going very well, I'd
put a puppy dog in it. . . .
                    —Norman Rockwell


**W**elcome to the best doggone guide to life ever written.
We, The Dogs, are your best friends, after all. So who
could give you better advice? Who better to tell you how to
live your life than the creatures who care most about you?

We know what it's like to be in the doghouse. We understand
how terrible it is to have an itch you can't reach. We realize
how much a good snack means.

That's why we've taken the time out of our busy dog days to
write this book.

We want to keep you out of the doghouse. We want to make
sure you're well-groomed. And we're determined to teach you
all the best ways to get great snacks!

So pull up an overstuffed pillow, turn around three times, and
settle in for a good read!

Woof!

# Basset Hound

*Let sleeping dogs lie. . . .*

—*Charles Dickens*

**WHO'S HOWLING?**

## ALL ABOUT ME.

**My Name:**

Basset Hound (in French that means "low set")

**My Average Height:**

14 inches

**My Average Weight:**

45 to 65 pounds

**My Coloring:**

Black, tan, white—in no particular order

## What I'm Trying to Say Is . . .

It might be a little hard to tell when we Basset Hounds are bowing down—you know, with our back legs up and our front legs flat on the ground—but with most dogs it's pretty easy to see that they're saying, "I want to play!" (We Basset Hounds usually just take naps instead.)

## Woofs of Wisdom

Put on a happy face! (Or if that seems like it might take too much energy, you might just want to take a nap. Sweet dreams!)

## Fur Fact

We, the Basset Hounds, cannot tell a lie. The father of our country, President George Washington, was a great man—and an owner of Basset Hounds.

## Four-Footed Funnies

Why did the Basset Hound bury his bone in the yard? *Because he was too short to put it up in the tree.*

## In the Doghouse. . .

Keep your head low and your nose to the ground. Trouble will sail right over your head! (Although you might also end up somewhere you've never been before by accident. That happens to us a lot and that's why our humans try not to let us wander away.)

## Food, Fur & You. . .

Always wash your ears . . . especially if you've recently stepped on them.

# Beagle

*To a dog, the whole world is a smell.*

**ALL ABOUT ME.**

**My Name:**

Beagle

**My Average Height:**

13 to 16 inches

**My Average Weight:**

20 to 25 pounds

**My Coloring:**

Tricolored—red, white, and orange—or lemon and white

###  What's That Smell?

We, the Beagles, are proud supersniffers. That's why we accidentally disappear sometimes. When a smell calls, we listen.

###  Woofs of Wisdom

Follow your nose! It always knows!

###  Fur Fact

Our name comes from the Celtic word *beag*. It means "small."

###  Things You Can Call Me:

Doggy. Dog. Cur. Puppy. Hound. Pup. Pooch. Canine. Mutt. Best Friend.

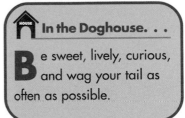

**In the Doghouse. . .**

Be sweet, lively, curious, and wag your tail as often as possible.

**Food, Fur & You. . .**

Are you tired of having to brush out snarls every day? Short hair hardly ever needs to be brushed and it's very attractive, especially if you grow it in several different colors at the same time.

# Bearded Collie

*In a perfect world, every dog would have a home and every home would have a dog.*

**ALL ABOUT ME.**

**My Name:**

Bearded Collie

**My Average Height:**

20 to 22 inches

**My Average Weight:**

40 to 60 pounds

**My Coloring:**

Black, steel blue, brown, or fawn with white markings

##  Howl-lo?

We know that some of you might think barking and howling are a little annoying. But remember, when we dogs bay at the moon, we're just trying to call our friends together. It may be a little loud, but it's cheaper than a phone.

## Woofs of Wisdom

The herd that plays together stays together.

## Fur Fact

Back in Scotland, we've been herding sheep for as long as we can remember. Folks will tell you we're really good at the job. Even though different flocks might meet one another during the day, we are really good at making sure we only take our own sheep home at night.

## Four-Footed Funnies

What do you get when you cross Lassie with a rose?
*A collie-flower!*

## In the Doghouse. . .

**W**hen getting your friends or family together, try not to nip at their heels. A polite request with a please and thank-you (or a quiet bark) will be more appreciated.

## Food, Fur & You. . .

**I**t's just rude to put your wet beard in someone's lap if you have a choice. But if your beard is just always a little wet because that's who you are, then it's okay.

# Bernese Mountain Dog

*Outside of a dog, a book is man's best friend, and inside a dog, it's too dark to read.*

—Groucho Marx

**WHO'S HOWLING?**

**ALL ABOUT ME.**

**My Name:**

Bernese Mountain Dog

**My Average Height:**

22 to 28 inches

**My Average Weight:**

70 to 110 pounds

**My Coloring:**

Black, rust, and white

##  Old Habits Die Hard

Ever wonder why we turn around before we lie down? Well, back in the old days when we were roaming wild, that was a really good way to trample down the grass or snow and make a cozy bed. We just haven't quite gotten out of the habit yet.

##  Woofs of Wisdom

If you want to make a friend, wag your tail instead of your tongue.

## Fur Fact

A Bernese Mountain Dog might live near you, but originally we're from Switzerland. You'll never believe how we got there! More than 2,000 years ago, Roman soldiers invaded Switzerland and brought us with them.

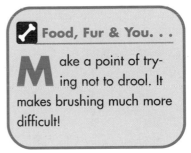

**In the Doghouse. . .**

It never hurts to say "I love you." It's hard for a person to stay mad at you when you're sitting in their lap—even if you happen to be quite furry and weigh 110 pounds.

**Food, Fur & You. . .**

Make a point of trying not to drool. It makes brushing much more difficult!

# Border Collie

*A barking dog is often more useful than a sleeping lion.*

—Washington Irving

**ALL ABOUT ME.**

**My Name:**

Border Collie

**My Average Height:**

18 to 22 inches

**My Average Weight:**

30 to 45 pounds

**My Coloring:**

Black and white, red and white, tricolor, black and gray, or all black

###  Sometimes the Smallest Things Are the Most Confusing. . . .

Make no mistake about it, we are herders. That's why we might snap at small children. Sometimes they just look an awful lot like sheep. We're just trying to get them to behave!

###  Woofs of Wisdom

Work hard. Sleep well.

### Fur Fact

The world's oldest dog was an Australian Cattle Dog named Bluey, who was more than 29 years old when he died.

### Movie Star Alert!

The dogs in *Babe* were Border Collies, too!

# Bulldog

**Bulldogs are adorable, with faces like toads that have been sat on.**

—*Colette*

## ALL ABOUT ME.

**My Name:**

Bulldog

**My Average Height:**

12 to 16 inches

**My Average Weight:**

49 to 53 pounds

**My Coloring:**

Brindle, white, red, fawn, or fallow

12

### Ohbay . . . oebae . . . obay . . . How Do You Spell That Word Again?

We, the Bulldogs, would like to make one thing perfectly clear—we do not think more slowly than other dogs. We just don't always care what's being said, so we don't answer. This is especially true when our humans say things like "sit," "come," and "roll over."

### Woofs of Wisdom

If you can't take the heat, stay out of the kitchen—or the backyard, or the doghouse, or anywhere else that isn't air-conditioned when it's hotter than 80 degrees outside!

### Fur Fact

Some folks think we're a little odd-looking, but there's a reason we look so funny. Every bit of us was bred to bait bulls! So go ahead and laugh if you want, but you'd look pretty funny, too, if you were only one foot tall and had the job of clamping onto a bull's nose with your mouth! As Winston Churchill once said, "The nose of the Bulldog has been slanted backwards so that he can breathe without letting go!"

### In the Doghouse. . .

If you don't move, you can't get in trouble.

### Food, Fur & You. . .

For a little relief from the heat during the summer, try putting powder in the folds of your skin and under your tail. We would also really advise against *any* exercise!

# Cocker Spaniel

*Children and dogs are as necessary to the welfare of the country as Wall Street and the railroads.*

—Harry S. Truman

**ALL ABOUT ME.**

My Name:

Cocker Spaniel

My Average Height:

14 to 16 inches

My Average Weight:

15 to 30 pounds

My Coloring:

Black, cream, dark red, brown, or brown with tan points

###  Read My Ears!

If you see a dog with its ears up, that means the dog is listening to something. If its ears are back, that probably means that the dog is scared.

###  Woofs of Wisdom

If you can't grow long hair, try growing long ears, like us!

###  Fur Fact

We are the smallest dog breed to be considered a sporting dog. Our name actually stems from our sporting–dog days. It comes from the woodcock, which is the bird we're really good at finding.

###  The Lady Is a Cocker Spaniel

Remember that lovely and elegant pooch who went for a spaghetti dinner with that mutt named Tramp? Well, Lady of *Lady and the Tramp* was one of us!

###  In the Doghouse. . .

**B**e sweet, because there's nothing worse than getting yelled at . . . for anything! We Cockers don't like to be yelled at. It makes us nervous and sad.

### Food, Fur & You. . .

**N**ever forget to clean your eyes. They are the windows to your little puppy soul, after all.

# Dachshund

*Dachshunds are ideal dogs for small children, as they are already stretched and pulled to such a length that a child cannot do much harm one way or another.*

—Robert Benchley

WHO'S HOWLING?

**ALL ABOUT ME.**

**My Name:**

Dachshund

**My Average Height:**

14 to 18 inches

**My Average Weight:**

20 pounds

**My Coloring:**

Tan, black, brown, gray, chestnut, or speckle-streaked

16

##  Our Eyes Are Bigger Than Our Stomachs. . . .

That's one way to explain why we bury bones. Back in the old days, when we were running wild . . . (okay, maybe Dachshunds weren't running wild, but you get our point!) Anyway, back then we often killed prey that was more than we could eat at one meal. So, since we couldn't hide the leftovers in a tree and didn't have refrigerators, we buried them. We've been doing it ever since!

## Woofs of Wisdom

Train your owner well.

## Fur Fact

We were bred to fight badgers in their dens!

## Hero Hall of Fame

### Great Dogs in History

| | | |
|---|---|---|
| Rin Tin Tin | Asta | Astro |
| Toto | Pluto | Lady |
| Sandy | Dino | Tramp |
| Lassie | Deputy Dawg | Goofy |
| Scooby-Doo | Blue | Beethoven |
| Benji | Odie | Wishbone |
| Shiloh | Huckleberry Hound | The Shaggy Dog |

### In the Doghouse. . .

**P**ick your friends carefully, if you're like us. We get irritated easily and the wrong company can end up getting bitten.

### Food, Fur & You. . .

**M**ay we suggest that the smaller the dog is, the thicker its sweater should be? We wee pups appreciate a little bit of clothing in the winter—and it's not all about looks!

17

# Dalmatian

*To err is human,*
*to forgive, canine.*

—Anonymous

**WHO'S HOWLING?**

## ALL ABOUT ME.

**My Name:**

Dalmatian (from Dalmatia along the Adriatic Sea!)

**My Average Height:**

19 to 24 inches

**My Average Weight:**

40 to 65 pounds

**My Coloring:**

White with black or liver-colored spots

##  Pardon Us!

When we stick out our tongues, please do not think we're being rude. It helps us cool off because our noses are like cooling systems! In fact, the longer the snout, the better it works.

##  Woofs of Wisdom

Getting along with all kinds of folks is always a good idea. We, the Dalmatians, first got our jobs at fire stations because we didn't argue with the horses who were pulling the wagons. Think first, bark later.

##  Fur Fact

As puppies we're all white. Spots come later. We are also the *only* breed of dog that can guarantee you spots!

## Collars & Other Accessories

**The Well-Appointed Pooch:** It's a well-known fact that back in the old days, a dog's collar could tell you how important that dog was. The collars might be made of gold, silver, white leather, or velvet! (A long, long time ago, Great Danes and Mastiffs used to be taken into battle wearing spiked collars and their own suits of armor.)

**In the Doghouse. . .**

Only speak when spoken to . . . or when you have to save the day with your super puppy strength and courage.

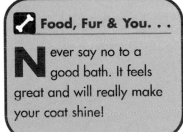

**Food, Fur & You. . .**

Never say no to a good bath. It feels great and will really make your coat shine!

# German Shepherd

*Always keep 'em guessing— wag your tail and bark at the same time!*

**ALL ABOUT ME.**

**My Name:**

German Shepherd

**My Average Height:**

22 to 26 inches

**My Average Weight:**

75 to 85 pounds

**My Coloring:**

Black and tan, sable, or all black

20

##  Fang Shui

Ever notice that a lot of us sleep with our heads facing north? We believe (and studies have shown) that it naturally improves circulation, metabolism, and slows our heart rates.

##  Woofs of Wisdom

Loyalty above all else!

##  Shepherd Hall of Fame

Rin Tin Tin, the famous movie star, was one of us!

##  Fur Fact

Our noses can find gas leaks in pipes that are buried 15 feet underground.

## Say What?

**The Lowdown on the Bow-Wow**

How many ways can you say d-o-g?

| | |
|---|---|
| Dog day afternoon | Dogged |
| Dog tired | Hot dog! |
| Doggone | Top dog |
| Dog-eared | Underdog |
| Dog breath | Snoop Doggy Dog |

**In the Doghouse. . .**

Keep yourself busy. Get a job. We suggest working as a watchdog, guide dog, sheep flocker, babysitter, bomb and drug detector, or doing search and rescue, police work, tracking, avalanche rescue, or even acting (like our hero, Rin Tin Tin).

**Food, Fur & You. . .**

Know your fur type. Are you rough-coated, long-rough-coated, or long-haired?

# Golden Retriever

*Every dog must have his day.*

—Jonathan Swift

**ALL ABOUT ME.**

**My Name:**

Golden Retriever

**My Average Height:**

20 to 24 inches

**My Average Weight:**

60 to 80 pounds

**My Coloring:**

Different shades of gold (of course)

22

## We Live to Please!

We are proud to announce that many of the most obedient dogs in the country are Golden Retrievers! That's because we just love to please our folks. That makes us excellent hunters, trackers, and guide dogs. We'll do anything for a pat on the head!

 ## Woofs of Wisdom

There is nothing more important than a gentle mouth. It makes you a fine duck retriever *and* a very good babysitter.

 ## Fur Fact

We dogs have been letting people live with us for 12,000 years.

## Four-Footed Funnies

What do you call a dog's kiss?
*A pooch smooch!*

## In the Doghouse. . .

Try not to be left alone. That can only lead to trouble. It's always best to be with your family if you really want to be happy and well-behaved.

## Food, Fur & You. . .

Tired of your plain old long, straight hair? Try feathering the stuff that grows on your legs and tail. We love it!

# Italian Greyhound

*Money can buy you a pretty nice dog, but it won't buy you the wag of its tail.*

**ALL ABOUT ME.**

**My Name:**

Italian Greyhound

**My Average Height:**

12 to 15 inches

**My Average Weight:**

6 to 10 pounds

**My Coloring:**

Solid gray, slate gray, cream, red, black

24

##  Smell Isn't Everything.

We are the smallest member of the family of dogs called *gazehounds*. That means we use our eyes to hunt. We hunt by sight, whereas most dogs hunt by smell.

##  Woofs of Wisdom

When all else fails . . . RUN!

##  Fur Fact

We Greyhounds were hanging out in ancient Egypt 5,000 years ago!

## What's in a Name?

You can call me *Mops Hond* (Dutch), *Mopsi* (Finnish), *Carlin Doguin* (Old French), *Smutmhadra* (Irish Gaelic for "stumpy dog"), *Mops Hund* (German), *Carlino* (Italian), *Doguillo* (Spanish), *Mops* (Swedish), or *Ha Ba Gou* (Old Chinese)— just don't call me late for dinner!

## 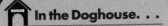 In the Doghouse. . .

It's important to know what you like and what you don't like. For example, if loud noises make you curl up and hide under the couch, then try to avoid loud households.

## Food, Fur & You. . .

Large amounts of chocolate can be dangerous (and even deadly) for us dogs—especially the kind of chocolate used for baking. Try giving us other kinds of snacks instead.

# Jack Russell Terrier

*If you can't decide between a Shepherd, a Setter, or a Poodle, get them all. . . . Adopt a mutt!*

—ASPCA

**ALL ABOUT ME.**

My Name:

Jack Russell Terrier

My Average Height:

10 to 14 inches

My Average Weight:

14 to 18 pounds

My Coloring:

White with reddish black, tan, or brown markings

26

## There's More Than One Way to Hunt a Fox

We don't dig just because it's fun (and it is). We dig because that's the way we hunt for foxes and other small animals. We dig them right out of their houses!

 ## Woofs of Wisdom

Fear is for cats.

 ## Fur Fact

Only two kinds of dogs have black tongues, the Shar-pei and the Chow Chow. The rest of us are in the pink!

## The -EST Report

**Largest:** Irish Wolf Hound

**Tallest:** Great Dane

**Heaviest:** Saint Bernard

**Smallest:** Chihuahua

**Highest:** Laika (Russian space dog—orbited in 1957)

**Quietest:** Basenji (the African wolf dog who can't bark)

**Best:** YOUR Dog

## In the Doghouse. . .

Keep your mouth to yourself. It's really hard to stop a fight once it starts.

## Food, Fur & You. . .

We're not saying we have a problem, but if you happen to notice someone has bad breath, you might want to consider getting them a teeth cleaning.

# Labrador Retriever

*Though the bark may be worse than the bite, most folks seem to prefer the bark.*

**ALL ABOUT ME.**

**My Name:**

Labrador Retriever

**My Average Height:**

21 to 24 inches

**My Average Weight:**

55 to 80 pounds

**My Coloring:**

Yellow, black, or chocolate

28

##  On Your Mark, Get Set . . .

Ever see one of us standing at the edge of the water with one paw up? Just getting ready for our next big move! It's as good as a runner crouched at the starting block. (Except it's more fun to swim.)

##  Woofs of Wisdom

No matter what the question is, the answer is always CHEWING!

## Fur Fact

You can call us Labradors now, but way back when we were taken to Newfoundland by explorers and settlers, we were called the Black Water Dog, the Lesser Newfoundland (excuse us!), and St. John's Dog.

## Work Experience

1800s: Jumped into icy waters around Newfoundland to haul fishing nets to shore.

## In the Doghouse. . .

When you accidentally chew something that turns out to be more important than you thought it was—like one half of a really expensive pair of shoes—go to the backyard right away and bury it. Get rid of the evidence!

## Food, Fur & You. . .

It's not polite to chew if you don't have enough for everyone. So unless you've snatched an extra shoe or glove or pillow, think about going to another room where you can chew by yourself.

# Old English Sheepdog

*The biggest dog has been a pup.*

—*Joaquin Miller*

## ALL ABOUT ME.

**My Name:**

Old English Sheepdog

**My Average Height:**

20 to 24 inches

**My Average Weight:**

60 to 100 pounds

**My Coloring:**

Blue, gray, or blue–gray with white markings

30

**Tell Me a Hairy Tail. . . .**

When some dogs curl up and go to sleep, they cover their noses with their tails. That's so they can keep their noses warm. We'd do the same thing if we had tails! Lucky for us, we have about ten pounds of extra-warm fur.

 **Woofs of Wisdom**

Shaggy is chic.

 **Fur Fact**

How many dogs do you know who have been given the job of herding reindeer? Count us in! That's what you can do when your fur is so warm that farmers use it to make blankets after the spring shearing. Cool job!

 **Four-Footed Funnies**

Which dog has long hair and never spends any money?
*An Old English Cheap Dog!*

**In the Doghouse. . .**

If you don't leave the couch, you can't get in trouble.

**Food, Fur & You. . .**

If your hair is so long that it hides your tail, think about getting rid of your tail. We did. That's why our nickname is Bobtails.

# Poodle

*No matter how little money and how few possessions you own, having a dog makes you rich.*

—Louis Sabin

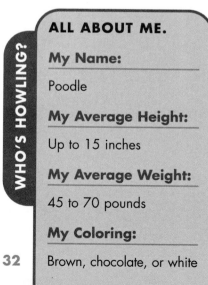

**WHO'S HOWLING?**

**ALL ABOUT ME.**

**My Name:**

Poodle

**My Average Height:**

Up to 15 inches

**My Average Weight:**

45 to 70 pounds

**My Coloring:**

Brown, chocolate, or white

##  It's Not All for Show!

We Poodles are famous for our poofy do's, but you should know we had some good reasons for those haircuts. The shaved parts lighten our load when we're swimming, and the furry parts are left furry to keep our joints and organs warm!

##  Woofs of Wisdom

Your hairdresser is your friend. Try not to growl at her.

Bonjour! Did you know we are the national dog of France? *Oui!*

##  Fur Fact

All dogs, including Poodles, are direct descendants of wolves. How do you like that?

## Did You Say Puddle?

The name Poodle probably came from the German word *pudel*. That means "one who plays in water."

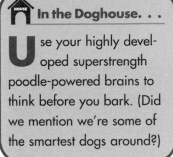

### In the Doghouse. . .

**U**se your highly developed superstrength poodle-powered brains to think before you bark. (Did we mention we're some of the smartest dogs around?)

### Food, Fur & You. . .

**P**om-poms are the perfect solution for naturally curly hair.

# Pug

*It's not the size of the dog in the fight, it's the size of the fight in the dog.*

—Mark Twain

**ALL ABOUT ME.**

**My Name:**

Pug

**My Average Height:**

10 to 14 inches

**My Average Weight:**

14 to 20 pounds

**My Coloring:**

Solid black, silver, or apricot fawn with black accents

WHO'S HOWLING?

34

##  Pug Motto

*Multum in Parvo* (a lot of dog in a small space)

##  Just DON'T Do It

Exercise is fine, but enough is enough—especially if you have a short muzzle. Our advice to you—if you start to wheeze, stop what you're doing and take a nap.

## Woofs of Wisdom

If you are going to bark, do it only when you must—and try to sound like a much bigger dog than you are.

## Fur Fact

Long live the Pugs! We're one of the oldest breeds of dogs. We go back as far as 400 B.C., and probably originally came from Asia.

### In the Doghouse. . .

Make friends with kings and queens and you'll always eat well—not to mention have statues made of you. (That's what we've done for hundreds of years!)

### Food, Fur & You. . .

Forget creams and lotions. If you're meant to be wrinkled, then you're going to be wrinkled. Be proud!

# Rottweiler

*If your dog doesn't like someone, you probably shouldn't, either.*

**ALL ABOUT ME.**

**My Name:**

Rottweiler

**My Average Height:**

22 to 27 inches

**My Average Weight:**

85 to 130 pounds

**My Coloring:**

Black with tan or mahogany markings

36

##  Just Doing Our Job, Ma'am.

We Rotties do not approve of biting. But one of the reasons that it happens sometimes is that we're very loyal to our families. We are always watching them. If it looks like someone is trying to hurt them, it's our job to stop that person.

##  Woofs of Wisdom

Protect the family! (And always ask permission before you pet someone else's dog.)

##  Fur Fact

We come from a breed of dogs called the Mastiff, which is why we're so big and strong. The world's heaviest and longest dog ever was an Old English Mastiff named Zorba. He weighed 343 pounds and was 8 feet, 3 inches long from his nose to his tail. Bow-WOW!

##  Names NOT to give a Rottweiler

| | | | |
|---|---|---|---|
| Fifi | Spot | Rover | Fluffy |
| Pee Wee | Junior | Snuggles | Lulu |

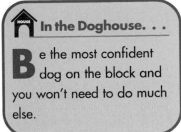

## In the Doghouse. . .

Be the most confident dog on the block and you won't need to do much else.

## Food, Fur & You. . .

It's a good idea to remove your tail before working on a farm. Long tails can get pretty gross when you're running around with cows. That's why we started having our tails cut off or "docked."

# Shih Tzu

A Pekingese is
not a pet dog;
he is an under-
sized lion.

—A.A. Milne

**ALL ABOUT ME.**

**My Name:**

Shih Tzu

**My Average Height:**

11 inches

**My Average Weight:**

9 to 16 pounds

**My Coloring:**

Black and white or
brown and white

38

##  A Tail Tale

There's more than one reason to wag a tail. Sometimes we wag it all over the place just because we're excited. But if you see a dog holding its tail low and only wagging it stiffly, that probably means that dog is scared. And, if you see a dog holding its tail up in the air and only wagging the tip, you can bet that dog is ready to get rough. So, walk away! That's what we do!

##  Woofs of Wisdom

Be polite and careful with me, and I will be polite and careful with you.

##  Fur Fact

Once upon a time, in the Far East, certain breeds of dogs like Pekingese and Japanese Chins were so important that they were given human servants.

### In the Doghouse. . .

Suggest to the people around you that it is a bad idea to sneak up on you, if you're not so good with being surprised. This might help you stop accidentally biting people.

### Food, Fur & You. . .

Manicures are not always about looking good—although we Shih Tzus do love a little color on our feet. But more important, long toenails can cause lots of feet problems. So check your toes (and our toes while you're at it)—and when you clip our toenails, watch out for the veins!

# Siberian Husky

*If you wish a dog to follow you . . . feed him.*

**WHO'S HOWLING?**

**ALL ABOUT ME.**

**My Name:**

Siberian Husky

**My Average Height:**

20 to 23 inches

**My Average Weight:**

35 to 69 pounds

**My Coloring:**

Black and white, gray and white, red and white, or just plain white

40

**Always Wear Your Snowshoes!**

If you have any questions about what to wear when it snows, you can ask us. We like to keep hair between our toes because it helps us grip the ice when we're pulling a sled. Mush!

 **Woofs of Wisdom**

Teamwork! Teamwork! Teamwork!

**Fur Fact**

At birth, we puppies can't see or hear, and can hardly smell! In fact, our eyesight isn't completely normal until we are about four weeks old.

**In the Doghouse. . .**

**K**eep a friend or some family nearby, because then you're less likely to get bored and lonely. Because if you're like us, being bored and lonely is one step away from being destructive and in trouble!

**Food, Fur & You. . .**

**W**ith the right coat, 76 degrees below zero is no big deal!

# West Highland White Terrier

*Try to be as good a person as your dog thinks you are.*

**ALL ABOUT ME.**

**My Name:**

West Highland White Terrier

**My Average Height:**

9 to 12 inches

**My Average Weight:**

13 to 22 pounds

**My Coloring:**

White

42

##  White Is Right!

You may wonder why – with all the colors in the world – we chose to be white. Well, back in the old days, we worked in Scotland, where there are lots of rocks. The white made it easier for us to be seen. But even more important, it made it harder for the hunters to mistake us for foxes!

##  Woofs of Wisdom

You can be small and even a little funny-looking as long as you have high(land) self-esteem!

##  Fur Fact

We see much better in dim light than humans do. That's because we have a special light-reflecting layer in our eyes that works like a mirror. That's why you might sometimes think our eyes glow.

##  Four-Footed Funnies

What dogs are best for sending telegrams?
*Wire-haired terriers!*

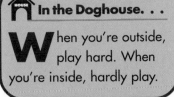

### In the Doghouse. . .

When you're outside, play hard. When you're inside, hardly play.

### Food, Fur & You. . .

If you happen to be all one color, try making your nose, lips, toenails, and eyeball rims another color—like black. We think it's a very attractive look. It will make your features stand out!

43

# Yorkshire Terrier

*The dog was created especially for children. . . .*

—Henry Ward Beecher

**ALL ABOUT ME.**

My Name:

Yorkshire Terrier

My Average Height:

6 to 7 inches

My Average Weight:

7 pounds

My Coloring:

Steel blue with tan head and legs

44

###  Dig It!

If you have an uncontrollable urge to dig, you might want to ask your folks if you're part terrier, like us. If you are, then you probably had ancestors who were supposed to dig for rodents and other cool stuff!

###  Woofs of Wisdom

If you think you might be a little short, just don't look in the mirror. If you don't know it, it doesn't matter!

###  Fur Fact

The smallest dog *ever* was one of us! The tiny Yorkie was two years old and only 2 1/2 inches tall, 3 1/2 inches long, and weighed 4 ounces! You could keep that Yorkie in a matchbox!

###  Sing Along with Us!

*If I can make it there, I'll make it anywhere . . .*
*It's up to me, New Yorkie, New Yorkie!!!*

---

### In the Doghouse. . .

**Y**ou can keep your nose out of trouble by covering it in very long fur. (However, that will not keep the rest of you out of trouble.)

### Food, Fur & You. . .

**E**ven a very small head can take a LOT of brushing —every day!

# People and their best friends . . . how do we compare?

| | PEOPLE | DOGS |
|---|---|---|
| Can hear a sound from . . . | 25 yards | 250 yards |
| Can detect sound wave vibrations . . . | 20,000 times/second | 30,000 times/second |
| Number of "smelling" cells in the nose . . . | 5,000,000 | 125–220,000,000 |
| Normal body temperature | 98.6° F | 101.2° F |
| Pregnancy | 9 months | 60 days |
| Ear muscles | half as many as dogs | twice as many as people |
| Heart rate | 79 to 80 beats/minute | 70 to 120 beats/minute |
| Physical maturity | 15 years old | 1 year old |

When the man waked up he said,
"What is wild dog doing here?"
And the woman said,
"His name is not wild dog anymore,
but the First Friend,
because he will be our friend
for always and always and always."
—Rudyard Kipling